A 30-Day Journal to Help You Experience and Spread Joy

JOY JOLT

A 30-Day Journal to Help You Experience and Spread Joy

Printed in the United States of America

ISBN:

Credits:
Copy Editor:
Kathleen Green Pothier, Positively Proofed,
   Plano, TX, info@positivelyproofed.com

Design:
Melissa Farr, Back Porch Creative,
   Frisco, TX, info@BackPorchCreative.com

INTRODUCTION

'm sitting in Starbucks writing these words. I love Starbucks. I love coffee. I have spent endless hours inside Starbucks locations all over the country. Some of my best creative ideas have come to me while sipping coffee at Starbucks. I have had incredibly meaningful conversations with friends and my children here. As much as I love coffee, I also love the idea of a place to enjoy it. Sociologists have identified the concept I'm describing as a "third place." A third place refers to a social surrounding that is different from the other obvious two – work and home. We need third places to regroup, relax, and enjoy friends.

When I'm at Starbucks, drinking coffee, enjoying meaningful work or conversations, I'm happy.

But what I've realized all these years of enjoying coffee – and more specifically coffee at Starbucks – is that this ritual brings me more than just happiness, it brings joy. Joy is deeper than just a feel-good morning drink. I've been a joy junkie for a long time. I seek that feeling, much like that jolt we experience when the caffeine of our favorite brew hits our neuropathways. BAM! You are awake. Aware. More mindful. Joy isn't the same as happiness (or caffeine). Happiness is usually a result of an outside force. Things, stuff, events bring happiness: an ice cream cone, a funny joke, a new sweater, shooting par or a promotion. But joy? Now that is the good stuff.

Joy comes from within. Joy takes that happy stuff and amplifies it. The amplification comes from deep-seated human elements. Joy uses memories, faith, stillness, and love to create a feeling that will stop you in your tracks. You will pause, even if that pause is only for a few seconds. And in those moments, joy – like a blanket that warms you from a chill – covers you, comforts you, and calms you.

"But Kathy, how does a cup of coffee get you to 'joy'?" you may be asking. Because I've used Starbucks as my third place for so long, the memories, faith, stillness, and love I've experienced drinking that coffee surface with a sip.

I can walk into my favorite Starbucks and memories rise like thick steam. I remember the time my daughter and I discussed her college applications. I witnessed her creativity and diligence.

While discussing raising Godly children or receiving counsel from best friends, my faith grew over our steaming cups. More than once, I prayed with friends at Starbucks or had an impromptu Bible study.

In moments when I needed a quiet place to contemplate both work and personal struggles, Starbucks and that coffee offered stillness. I had four children in seven years, and as soon as the kids were on the bus and the pre-school drop-off was made, I would often sit quietly at Starbucks. I refer to that time as my therapy.

And love. Yes, I found love at Starbucks. I met my husband in line. (Not ONLINE!) We were Starbucks buddies back before smartphones kept everyone's heads down while waiting for their lattes. We seemed to always arrive around the same time. Over a period of about seven years, we chatted in line, learned about each other's families, and joked about the over-caffeinated baristas. Then during one of those conversations, we learned that we were both going through divorce. We eventually drank a cup of coffee together.

Memories, faith, stillness, and love collide with moments in my day to fill up my joy cup. And those moments often arrive with a JOLT. Those collisions can't be calculated or predicted. They just happen. But they happen more often when we are aware that ***joy is waiting on us*** – waiting for us to recognize it, and to remove the constricts that keep it from pouring out. ***Joy is waiting to JOLT you.***

I wrote this book to help you find out what fills your joy cup. I wrote it to help you become more aware of the moments when an event, a person, a song, a food, and so much more can trigger joy. It's the deeper version of the moment. Joy rests deep in your soul, and it begs to come out. Daily, hourly – right now!

Why is joy so important? In a world full of hurt, sadness, and uncertainty, we need more joy. Joy doesn't cost anything. It is infinite. After we find joy within ourselves, we get to do what joy really asks of us: We get to spread it.

Like a jolt of electricity from a lightning bolt, a Joy Jolt has power … power to expand.

This book will help you identify, delight in, and spread joy. It is designed to allow you to go deeper each day and find those moments that can expand to joy. Use it for thirty days and I believe you will find more Joy Jolts than you could have ever imagined.

JOY JOLT

A moment that causes
pause-worthy delight,
which can spread to others.

How to use the daily Joy Jolt Journal

Read the daily prompt and see if you can either experience joy that day or go back to a memory that involves the prompt. Memories can bring us to a joyful place as easily as a current experience.

Fill in the Joy Jolt section with a few thoughts about the prompt. When did you experience it? Who was there? How long did the feeling of joy last?

Think about how you could share a bit of the joy you felt with someone else. Would you send a picture? A text? An invitation? A word of encouragement?

At the end of thirty days, take time to fill out the final reflections. Return to this section often. Use it to remind yourself of your favorite ways to receive the Joy Jolts and how you intend to share joy.

Nature

Looking at a lake, watching a bird in flight, observing a pattern of frost on a window.

The beauty of nature is everywhere. Take a moment to acknowledge something in nature today. Can you connect that with a memory? Does it take you deeper in your faith?

Joy Jolt Reflection:

____

____

____

How can I spread joy today?

____

____

____

Achievement

A certification, a promotion, a health goal.

You have accomplished a lot in your life. When did you accomplish something that made you proud? Did your child reach a goal that was unexpected? Is there something that you could do today that you've been putting off? Can you congratulate someone today on their achievement?

Joy Jolt Reflection:

____

____

____

How can I spread joy today?

____

____

____

Events

A concert, a children's soccer game, a birthday party.

Think about a time when you were at an event. Did you feel love for someone else at that event? Do you remember their laugh? At the next event you attend, can you be more mindful of the experience? Find a picture of an event you attended and send it to someone who was there. Tell them what that event meant to you.

Joy Jolt Reflection:

____

____

____

How can I spread joy today?

____

____

____

Elders

Parents, grandparents, residents or patients.

Elders offer wisdom and have a wealth of experiences. How has an elder affected your life? Did they give you great advice? Did they pass along a skill, recipe or memento? Can you share their wisdom with someone else today? Can you thank them?

Joy Jolt Reflection:

____

____

____

How can I spread joy today?

____

____

____

Joy Jolt
Day 5

Destinations

A restaurant, a road trip, a hidden treasure near home.

Exploring new locations opens our eyes and hearts to more joy. Can you go somewhere today and experience new sights, smells, and sounds? What is different about this new destination? Can you think of someone you could share this spot with? Did you meet anyone new there?

Joy Jolt Reflection:

____

____

____

How can I spread joy today?

____

____

____

Childhood Friend

Who was that person whom you giggled with, played after school with, or tried out for the team with?

Those more innocent relationships revolved around fun activities and shared interests. What did you do with your friend? What made the day the best day ever? Can you reach out to that person and ask them, "Do you remember….?"

Joy Jolt Reflection:

____

____

____

How can I spread joy today?

____

____

____

Compliments

She told you she liked your coat. He acknowledged the extra effort you added to the project.

Compliments and acknowledgements can stick with us for a long time. We often remember exactly how we felt when we were acknowledged. Who gave you a compliment that still fills you with joy when you think about it? Can you spark joy in someone today with a positive affirmation?

Joy Jolt Reflection:

____

____

____

How can I spread joy today?

____

____

____

A Season

Winter, spring, summer or fall – each season has the ability to give us moments of joy. Which is your favorite?

Does a snow-covered tree make you pause in delight? Do you have joy-filled memories of swimming at your grandparents' lake? Can you step outside right now and allow the scene around you to uncover joy?

Joy Jolt Reflection:

____

____

____

How can I spread joy today?

____

____

____

Kindness

Rescuing a stray kitten, taking food to an elder neighbor, finishing a task for someone at work.

We have so many daily opportunities to show kindness. The joy that kindness brings almost always flows both ways. How could you create a kindness culture in the workplace? Whom do you know that could use some more kindness? When you see kindness, what does that joy feel like?

Joy Jolt Reflection:

____

____

____

How can I spread joy today?

____

____

____

Art

Music, dance, sculpture, and paintings are just a few of the many art forms that surround us.

We can participate in the art, or we can observe. Either way, the rhythms, colors or textures can ignite joy in us. What art do you see around you today? Is the art beautiful or does it make you think differently? What form of art brings you joy?

Joy Jolt Reflection:

____

____

____

How can I spread joy today?

____

____

____

Joy Jolt
Day 11

Family

Small, large, easy, complex.

We cannot change our families, but we can look for joy in each relationship. For some relationships, that is hard. In that case, the joy may be in recognizing how you have moved through difficulty. Do you have a favorite family tradition? Could you reach out to a sibling today and share a joy-filled memory?

Joy Jolt Reflection:

____

____

____

How can I spread joy today?

____

____

____

Physical Touch

Holding your love's hand, playing "this little piggy" on your child's toes, destressing during a massage.

Human physical touch has the power to convey what words can't. Whom can you literally touch today and convey that joy?

Joy Jolt Reflection:

____

____

____

How can I spread joy today?

____

____

____

Animals

Dogs, cats, a bunny in the garden.

Whether you have a beloved pet or feed the deer in your yard, animals can cause us to stop and be mindful in the moment. What does your pet do that brings you joy? Can you take a picture of an animal in nature and share it?

Joy Jolt Reflection:

____

____

____

How can I spread joy today?

____

____

____

Sunset/Sunrise

At the beach, off your back deck or through the kitchen window.

Do you feel the presence of a greater power – God? – while witnessing a beautiful sunrise or sunset? Pausing for the start or passing of the day can fill us with joy. When did you last experience that joyful feeling?

Joy Jolt Reflection:

____

____

____

How can I spread joy today?

____

____

____

Joy Jolt
Day 15

Caregiving

A baby, an elder, a sick friend.

When we step into the role of caregiving, we often feel the joy of human connection and empathy. Whom have you cared for in your life? Do you allow yourself to be cared for? How did the joy surface in that experience? Can you express gratitude today for someone who took time to care for you?

Joy Jolt Reflection:

____

____

____

How can I spread joy today?

____

____

____

Colors

A yellow rose, a bright-orange 1969 Mustang convertible, a basket of deep-green peppers at the farmers market.

Colors ignite feelings and often a memory. Pause today and look more than a few seconds at a favorite color. What does it remind you of? How could that color be used more often in your surroundings?

Joy Jolt Reflection:

____

____

____

How can I spread joy today?

____

____

____

Food

Dark chocolate cake, a ripe apple picked off a tree, your mother's cheesy potatoes.

Food is one of our greatest joys. Besides the nutritional value, food elicits memories and can hold us in the moment to savor it, and we often enjoy it with the people we love. What food will you go out of your way to find, eat, or make? Could you share with others today the joy that food brings you?

Joy Jolt Reflection:

____

____

____

How can I spread joy today?

____

____

____

A Show

A binge-worthy series, a live concert, a movie at the theater.

Entertainment from shows – in person or on the couch – can transport us to different locations, help us tap into our feelings or just let us release some stress. What show recently allowed you to experience joy – in the story, or the acting or the time spent watching it with someone you love?

Joy Jolt Reflection:

____

____

____

How can I spread joy today?

____

____

____

Movement

Saturday morning yoga class, a walk through your favorite park, completing a 5K.

Physical movement and exercise not only release dopamine (the happy hormone) but can also release your joy. What movement – pent up while you sat all day – unleashes your joy? Could you commit to this movement more often? Who could you exercise with and share that joy?

Joy Jolt Reflection:

____

____

____

How can I spread joy today?

____

____

____

Reconnecting

A distant cousin, your first love, a former co-worker.

At one point in your life, a certain person was very significant, but you lost touch. Reconnecting with that person can bring back some of the joy you felt when they were in your life. The connection may mean going through a photo album or reaching out. How can you reconnect with a special person and gather some of the joy from a past relationship?

Joy Jolt Reflection:

____

____

____

How can I spread joy today?

____

____

____

Joy Jolt
Day 21

Smells

Freshly cut grass, chocolate chip cookies baking, climbing into a new car.

Smell, like our four other basic senses, has the capacity to stir up joyful memories. Aroma can stop us in our tracks and make us inhale deeply. What odor will cause you to pause and enjoy the smell? What does that smell remind you of? How can that smell connect to joy?

Joy Jolt Reflection:

____

____

____

How can I spread joy today?

____

____

____

Comfort

A warm blanket on your lap, your favorite jeans or yoga pants, a perfect warm shower.

When we feel physically comfortable, our barriers to joy are released. How does joy feel when you are comfortable? Can you incorporate more comfort in your days? How can you share that comfort with someone else?

Joy Jolt Reflection:

____

____

____

How can I spread joy today?

____

____

____

Joy Jolt
Day 23

Hobbies

Woodworking, photography, birdwatching, gardening.

What you do in your free time can offer many Joy Jolts. Do you enjoy that hobby with someone else? Or does it bring you peace in solitude? How can you use your free time to unveil more moments of joy?

Joy Jolt Reflection:

____

____

____

How can I spread joy today?

____

____

____

Friends

Team friends, work friends, neighborhood friends.

You may have a long list of friends or just a handful of very special people. Whoever your friends are, they most likely share things in common with you, and they understand you and your joys and struggles. What ways does joy bubble up when you spend time with your friends? Could you share more moments of joy with them?

Joy Jolt Reflection:

____

____

____

How can I spread joy today?

____

____

____

Surprises

An unexpected visitor, a text from someone whom you haven't heard from in a while, a gift you weren't expecting.

Most surprises bring joy because we don't have time to think or plan. We don't overprocess. What was the best surprise you ever received? How can you connect with that surprised feeling more often? Could you surprise someone today?

Joy Jolt Reflection:

____

____

____

How can I spread joy today?

____

____

____

Work

Team meetings, finishing projects, serving others, a promotion.

Whatever work you do, it should have moments of joy. We forget that joy should be a part of work. While at work, take a moment to slow down just for a minute and ask yourself what part of your vocation is joyful. How can you create more joy in your work?

Joy Jolt Reflection:

____

____

____

How can I spread joy today?

____

____

____

Laughing

A silly dog video, a sitcom sketch, your toddler putting stickers on the cat.

Laughter is the cousin of joy. A laugh can physically move us and give us pause for joy to sneak in. What makes you laugh? Do you laugh often? How can you put more laughter and play into your day?

Joy Jolt Reflection:

____

____

____

How can I spread joy today?

____

____

____

Faith

Daily meditation, a prayer of gratitude, a life-guiding force.

Faith is our individual relationship with God, or a higher power. Giving up control to that power allows us to be present in joy – joy in the mystery, joy in gratitude. How does your faith fill you with joy? What practices could you add to your day to connect with your God and to experience joy?

Joy Jolt Reflection:

____

____

____

How can I spread joy today?

____

____

____

Teams

Your daughter's soccer team, the project team at your work, your favorite football team.

The camaraderie that comes from being either on a team or sharing a passion for a team bonds us with others. Winning, competing or learning help us uncover the joy of teamwork. What team experiences bring you joy? Can you share with a team member how they have impacted your life?

Joy Jolt Reflection:

____

____

____

How can I spread joy today?

____

____

____

Giving

A birthday present, volunteering at a food bank, donating on a GoFundMe page.

Giving of time, talent or treasures is a precious way to share and receive joy. What do you most like to give? How have you seen joy manifest when you give? Can you create daily practices to give more often?

Joy Jolt Reflection:

____

____

____

How can I spread joy today?

____

____

____

YOU!

Your reflection in the mirror, your thoughts, your soul.

You are a beautiful and glorious creation. How do your thoughts, words or heart create joy, express it, and spread it? What are your attributes that release joy? How are you sharing that joy?

Joy Jolt Reflection:

____

____

____

How can I spread joy today?

____

____

____

Final Reflections

Where did you find more joy in the past thirty days?

____

____

____

____

____

____

____

____

____

____

____

Final Reflections

What specific areas of your life bring you the most joy?

____

____

____

____

____

____

____

____

____

____

Final Reflections

How do you like to spread joy?

____

____

____

____

____

____

____

____

____

____

____

Final Reflections

What do you intend to do to continue your
Joy Jolt Journey?

____

____

____

____

____

____

____

____

____

____

Final Jolt

Life is not always easy. Some days joy will be difficult to cultivate. If you have read any of my previous books, or you have heard me speak, you may know that I lost a child. My youngest daughter of four children was born with degenerative mitochondrial dysfunction. She was given a two-year life expectancy. When I felt like the joy had drained away after her diagnosis, I dove deep into the meaning of joy. I realized that joy is a fruit of the spirit, meaning it is already in us. We all get it. No one is exempt from joy, and no one can steal your joy. But we need to allow joy to surface, even when life is difficult.

Let the JOY JOLTS you have listed help you let the joy out. Merritt, my daughter, lived until she was twenty! She had severe disabilities, she never spoke, walked or had any capacity to function on her own. But like the middle name I gave her before she was even born, Merritt JOY spread joy to others every day.

Big, grandiose gestures aren't what allow joy to come out; it's the quiet mindfulness to focus on the moment. I wish for an abundance of joy to surface for you each day.

If life feels really hard, please reach out for help. Do not diminish the importance of your mental health. A state-by-state listing of mental well-being organizations can be found here: https://www.thenationalcouncil. org/get-involved/members/

About Kathy Parry

have a list of credentials, but that isn't what I want you to know about me. I'm a caregiver. I care about people, especially those who need extra care. I'm also a chronic over-giver, and I'm working on that. What I have learned (and not from my degrees or certifications) is that we all will need care at some point in our lives. I believe it is an honor to care for another human, and I'm learning to let others take care of me. Caring brings me joy.

When I'm not on the road speaking and training, I live at a lake in Ohio with my husband, Bryan, and our mini-Bernadoodle, Phil. Our combined eight children are out in the world learning how joy shows up in their lives.

Please feel free to connect with me on the socials. And please, share your Joy Jolts with me.

Kathy@KathyParry.com
www.KathyParry.com

Work With Kathy to Bring a Joy Jolt to Your Organization

Joy junkie Kathy Parry is a nationally recognized keynote speaker and trainer and author of five additional books.

Would you like Kathy to present at your next conference, leadership meeting or team event?

Are you ready to help your team, organization or association re-energize or find more joy? Do you want your audience or team to be super-charged? Email Kathy Parry at Kathy@KathyParry.com to schedule a discovery phone call.

Kathy's topics engage participants and give actionable takeaways. Her sessions – *Rubber Band Resilience, Workforce Power UP*, and *Joy Jolt* – are perfect for conference keynotes, leadership retreats, and workshops.

To learn more about Kathy's programs, visit **www.KathyParry.com** or email Kathy at **Kathy@KathyParry.com**

www.ingramcontent.com/pod-product-compliance
Lightning Source LLC
Chambersburg PA
CBHW041216150726
48006CB00016B/2268